SHIRE NATURAL H

CU00970844

GRASSES

PATRICIA HAWLEY

CONTENTS

Cover: *One of the commonest grasses of fields and open places, smooth meadow-grass (Poa pratensis).*

Series editor: Jim Flegg.

Copyright © 1989 by Patricia Hawley. First published 1989. Number 44 in the Shire Natural History series. ISBN 0 7478 0026 X. All rights reserved. No part of this publication may be reproduced or transmitted in any form or by any means, electronic or mechanical, including photocopy, recording, or any information storage and retrieval system, without permission in writing from the publishers, Shire Publications Ltd, Cromwell House, Church Street, Princes Risborough, Aylesbury, Bucks HP17 9AJ, UK.

Printed in Great Britain by C. I. Thomas & Sons (Haverfordwest) Ltd, Press Buildings, Merlins Bridge, Haverfordwest, Dyfed.

Introduction

Grasses provide the background to more colourful plants, both in the countryside and in our gardens. Although well kept lawns can be a source of enormous pride, they are of minor importance compared to the vast areas of land throughout the world covered with natural grasslands or cultivated cereal crops. When the dependence of foraging and grazing livestock on grasses is considered, it is obvious that no plant group is of greater economic importance than the grass family (the Gramineae, sometimes known by the alternative botanical name, Poaceae). This book shows how these immensely important plants are as diverse and captivating as any other flowering plants and introduces some of the commoner British species.

Grasses belong to the Monocotyledons, one of the two main subdivisions of the flowering plants, which take their name from the single seed leaf (or cotyledon) produced by each seed when it germinates. Other characteristics include parallel-veined leaves and floral parts which are generally grouped in threes. Many monocotyledonous families have conspicuous flowers with well developed petals, such as the water plantains and their relatives (Alismataceae), the flowering rushes (Butomaceae), the lilies (Liliaceae) and the irises (Iridaceae). These showy flowers are usually pollinated by insects attracted to the conspicuous blooms.

A number of specialised families of monocotyledons have evolved reduced petals. Their relatively inconspicuous flowers are less attractive to pollen- or nectar-gathering insects and their pollen is dispersed by the wind instead. Most of these superficially similar, grass-like, wind-pollinated families are included in a group of plants called the Glumiflorae. The grass family, with some 620 genera, is not only one of the largest plant families but in terms of individual plants is the most numerous in the world. Most grass genera are tropical, but even so about sixty genera are found in Britain, represented by more than 150 species. Tropical grasses may be of much greater stature than those of temperate Europe. Of these, the bamboos are even woody, although their hollow, hardened stems differ in structure from the solid wood of dicotyledonous trees.

Grasses are very familiar plants, but distinguishing them from the other families of wind-pollinated monocotyledons can be quite difficult (figure 8). The sedges (Cyperaceae) are particularly close in general appearance but can be recognised by the three-ranked arrangement of their leaves around solid, triangular stems. The leaves of sedges are not jointed at the base like those of grasses and do not form open-sided sheaths around the stems. A few sedges, like the cotton grasses (*Eriophorum* species), have common names that reflect their appearance and suggest membership of the Gramineae. The rushes (Juncaceae) are common in waterlogged places and are also grass-like but have minute, brownish, rather scaly petals. Like those of sedges, the stems of rushes are solid or filled with a white, spongy pith. One group, the wood-rushes (*Luzula* species), is particularly grass-like in appearance, having flattened leaf blades. When they are not in flower wood-rushes can best be recognised by the long, delicate whitish hairs fringing their leaves. The reed-maces (*Typha* species), sometimes known as bulrushes, are placed in a distinct family of their own. Although their leaves are grass-like, the familiar bulrush inflorescences have male flowers above and female below. In most grasses individual flowers are bisexual, although corn cobs (*Zea mais*) provide an unusual but well known example of entirely unisexual inflorescences.

The best characters for recognising grasses are their hollow stems, which are usually only solid at the joints, or nodes; their linear leaves, with flattened blades arising from jointed bases and sheaths encircling the stem; and their flowers, lacking petals and borne in spikelets, either singly or in groups.

Biology

The grass plant consists of a fibrous root system arising from a very compact stem,

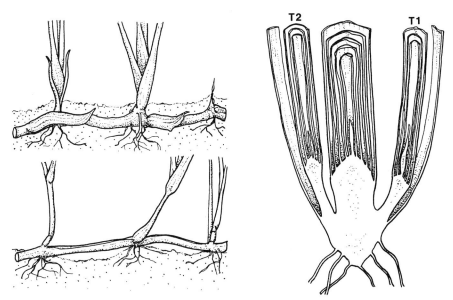

1. (left). *Spreading, horizontal stems of grasses. (Above) Underground rhizome of marram grass (Ammophila arenaria) compared with the stolon of creeping bent (Agrostis stolonifera) (below).*
2. (right). *Section through the culm of wheat (Triticum aestivum) showing two side shoots (T1 and T2) formed successively by tillering.*

known as a culm. In larger grasses such as maize the base of the stem may be supported by spreading prop roots, like miniature versions of the buttress roots of some tropical trees. Some grasses have horizontal stems by means of which the plant can grow and spread extensively without having to set seed (figure 1). Two types of horizontal stem may be distinguished: green stems which have complete leaves at their nodes (stolons) and white or brownish stems without leaves that grow deeper in the soil (rhizomes). Both types can easily be seen and compared on sand dunes where the spreading rhizomes of marram grass (*Ammophila arenaria*) and the stolons of creeping bent (*Agrostis stolonifera*) are often exposed by the wind. In more stable habitats the considerable extent to which many grasses spread by stolons and rhizomes is much less obvious. The culm of grasses is an unusual stem in that it does not normally elongate until the onset of flowering. The extremely reduced length of the culm protects the growing regions of the grass plant from grazing animals. The fact that the leaves of grasses extend from basal

areas of actively dividing cells adds to their resistance to grazing: since the growing parts are close to ground level, damage is less likely to occur. The plant begins to take the risk of extending upwards only when it is about to flower. During their vegetative growth before flowering begins, many species of grass also increase by a process known as tillering. New buds arise at the base of leaves and grow into independent shoots, or tillers, from which new root systems soon begin to develop. Tillering gives rise to dense clumps of short leafy stems (figure 2) and can be particularly easily seen in the early growth of most cereal crops.

The leaves of grasses arise from tightly rolled, sheathing bases which clasp the stems. Above this the leaf blade diverges at a well marked junction where a thin membranous structure, the ligule, is present. Details of the junction between sheath and blade provide many useful characters for identifying grasses (figure 3). The sheath itself may be a continuous, closed cylinder splitting open just below the blade, as in the bromes (*Bromus*

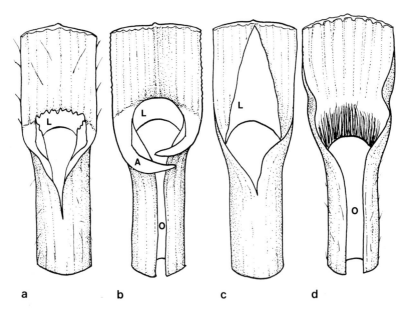

3. *Characters of the leaf bases of grasses: a, upright brome (Bromus erectus): leaf sheath closed, ligule (L) slightly toothed, auricles absent; b, giant fescue (Festuca gigantea): leaf sheath open (O), ligule not toothed, auricles (A) present; c, floating sweet-grass (Glyceria fluitans): leaf sheath closed, ligules lanceolate, auricles absent; d, common cord-grass (Spartina anglica): leaf sheaths open, ligule a ring of hairs, auricles absent.*

4. *Cross-sections of grass leaves showing motor-tissue involved in leaf rolling (motor-tissues stippled, conducting tissues shaded in black): a, cocksfoot (Dactylis glomerata) with a single band of motor cells; b, smooth meadow-grass (Poa pratensis) with two bands of motor cells; c, Timothy (Phleum pratense) with numerous bands of motor cells; d, marram grass (Ammophila arenaria) with permanently rolled leaves.*

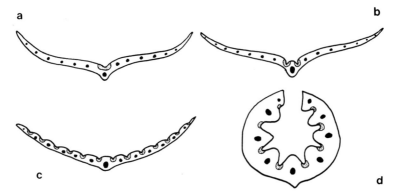

species), the sweet-grasses (*Glyceria* species) or the melicks (*Melica* species); or it may be open along one side as in the majority of grasses. The sheath may vary in colour from the usual pale green to yellowish in crested dog's-tail (*Cynosurus cristatus*), purplish brown in meadow foxtail (*Alopecurus pratensis*) or pink-veined in Yorkshire fog (*Holcus lanatus*). The leaf blade may narrow gradually into

4

the sheath or may be extended into a pair of pointed projections called auricles. The ligule is one of the most useful diagnostic vegetative features and shows wide variation in form between different grasses. Ligules differ in length, stiffness and in their margins, which may be smooth or toothed. In a few grasses, including the cord-grasses (*Spartina* species), purple moor-grass (*Molinia caerulea*) and common reed (*Phragmites communis*), the ligules are reduced to a ring of hairs.

The shape of the blade itself is often useful in identification. The tip of the blade may be characteristically pointed or blunt, and the blade may be tightly rolled or more or less flattened. The flattened leaves of some species may, however, fold or roll up during dry weather to conserve moisture. Leaves which change shape in this way do so because of rows of special enlarged thin-walled cells lying along their upper surfaces (figure 4). Cocksfoot (*Dactylis glomerata*) has a single row of this special 'motor-tissue' along the centre vein and the meadow-grasses (*Poa* species) have two rows. In these species the leaves become folded as moisture is lost from the motor-tissue causing its cells to shrink in volume. Rolling of the leaves occurs in grasses such as cat's-tails (*Phleum* species) and dog's-tails (*Cynosurus* species) which have more numerous bands of motor-tissue. Permanently rolled leaves are found in other grasses, particularly those of arid environments. In marram grass (*Ammophila arenaria*) the tightly rolled leaves have a cylindrical cross-section which prevents water being lost by evaporation from the microscopic pores (or stomata) on the upper surface of the leaf.

FLOWERS

Whilst vegetative characteristics can be very useful in the identification of grasses, the distinctions between genera and species are often based upon features of their flowers. Grass flowers (or florets) (figure 5) are highly reduced structures; each has one to six pollen-producing stamens (depending on the species) and a single ovary containing one ovule and topped by two feathery stigmas. The feathery stigmas are adapted to catching wind-blown pollen and the stamens have pollen sacs which are loosely attached to their long stalks, or filaments, to facilitate the release of pollen into the air. These fertile parts of the flower are accompanied by two small scale-like structures called lodicules which are sterile and correspond to highly reduced petals. The ovary, stamens and lodicules are enclosed by a pair of strongly curved scales, also sterile, which complete the structure of the individual grass flower, or floret. The inner scale is called the palea and the outer the lemma. The tips of some lemmas are extended into projections called awns, the presence or absence of which is often a valuable guide to the identity of a grass. The organisation of florets varies little between different groups of grasses, although the number of stamens and lodicules can vary.

The arrangement of florets into flower heads, or inflorescences, may differ enormously and is highly characteristic. Florets themselves are grouped into clusters called spikelets (figure 9), the basic units of which combine to make up the various kinds of grass inflorescence (figure 6). At the base of each spikelet are two scale-like bracts known as glumes. Often the spikelet is so densely packed together that only the glumes are obvious until it is teased apart and examined closely. A spikelet may consist of one floret, as in the bents (*Agrostis* species) and the cat's-tails (*Phleum* species), up to about twenty in the false-bromes (*Brachypodium* species). The simplest type of inflorescence is the spike, in which spikelets without stalks are attached along an unbranched central axis. If the florets have stalks but are otherwise organised as in a spike the inflorescence is called a raceme. When the spikelets are borne on a repeatedly branching axis this is known as a panicle. Panicles can differ in appearance depending on the length of the stalks and distance between the branches. The panicles of the bents (*Agrostis* species) and meadow-grasses (*Poa* species) are loose whereas those of Timothy or common cat's-tail (*Phleum pratense*) are so compact that the inflorescence looks rather like a spike. Close inspection is sometimes needed to determine whether

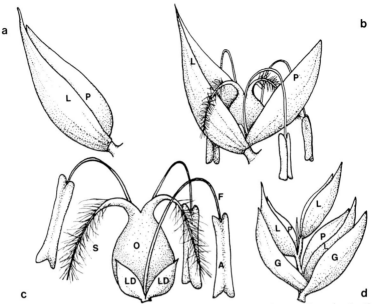

5. *Grass flowers: a, closed floret showing lemma (L) and palea (P); b, open floret; c, detail of floret with lemma and palea removed, showing lodicules (LD), the stamens consist of filaments (F) and anthers (A), the ovary (O) has two feathery styles (S); d, structure of a spikelet containing three florets surrounded by the two glumes (G).*

or not an inflorescence is branching.

The flowers of grasses are so small that it is rarely possible to examine their details with the naked eye, so a hand lens of x10 magnification is extremely useful. A few grasses have relatively large flowers, and wild oat (*Avena fatua*) is an ideal species for familiarisation with the basic construction of the grass flower. Its loose panicles have pendulous spikelets, each with two or three florets, and the lemmas are easily identified by the single conspicuous awn, an elongated projection which each has at its tip. Whether awns are present or not is often a valuable guide to the identity of a grass.

LIFE CYCLE

The seed, or grain, of a grass is shed as a complicated structure known as a caryopsis. Each caryopsis contains an embryo with energy-rich reserves surrounded by a thin layer formed from the hardened wall of the ovary and is usually dispersed with the lemma and palea still attached. Many cultivated cereals, such as wheat (*Triticum* species) and its close relative rye (*Secale cereale*), have been selected to produce varieties in which the caryopsis separates from the lemma and palea during threshing. When the caryopsis is shed the embryo inside is dormant, its cells being dehydrated and inactive. During germination (figure 7) water is absorbed and the embryo cells begin to divide actively and grow again until the wall of the grain splits open. The first root then emerges and grows downwards, soon producing lateral branches and establishing a supply of water for the growing seedling. Soon afterwards the single seed leaf emerges and normal foliage leaves begin to develop. These grow up through the seed leaf and the normal organisation of the culm becomes established. The grass plant continues to grow by the formation of new leaves, perhaps accompanied by tillering and the formation of additional roots.

A different pattern of growth is triggered when conditions of day length and temperature bring about flowering. The apex of the culm begins to produce a young inflorescence, rolled tightly inside

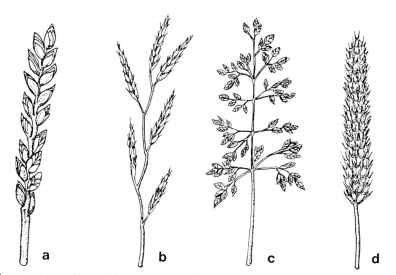

6. *Common types of grass inflorescence: a, spike; b, raceme; c, panicle; d, compact panicle with short branches giving a spike-like appearance.*

7. *The life cycle of a grass. The mature plant (A) produces pollen grains (B), which germinate on the feathery styles (C). Fertilisation leads to the formation of the grain (D), which germinates (E, F) to produce a seedling (G), which grows vegetatively by tillering (H) until flowering shoots are eventually produced (A).*

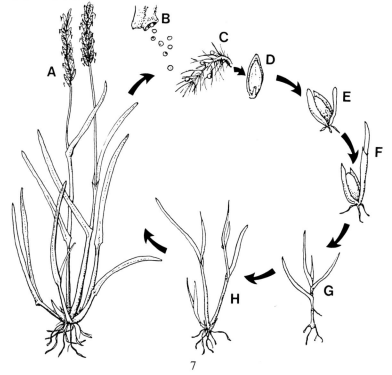

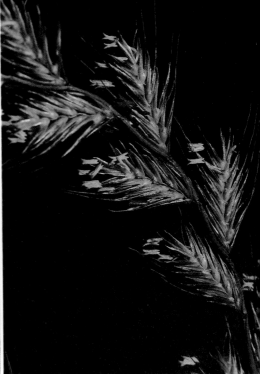

8 (left). *A damp meadow dominated by Alopecurus pratensis, growing with Juncus species.*
9 (right). *Spikelets of Italian rye-grass (Lolium multiflorum) showing conspicuous awns and pendulous anthers.*

the final leaf. This leaf is known in cereals as the flag leaf and protects the developing inflorescence during a period of extension of the culm. This extension takes place because the onset of flowering promotes the division of cells at each node of the culm. A rapid period of growth occurs during which the developing flower is raised well clear of the vegetative leaves of the grass. When the flowers open they are then held in an advantageous position for the release of pollen.

Two of the earliest flowering species are sweet vernal-grass (*Anthoxanthum odoratum*) and meadow fox-tail (*Alopecurus pratensis*), which usually begin to flower in late April. Most British grasses flower between May and July but a few species flower well into November. At the height of the flowering season hay-fever sufferers are often very badly affected by the large amounts of grass pollen in the air (figure 10). The pollen carries proteins to which the sufferers are allergic. Although the flowering period of each species may extend for many weeks, individual grass florets open only for about a week. During this time the flower opens for a few hours each day, often at quite specific times. In most species the female parts reach maturity first and the feathery stigmas spread outwards to catch pollen from the air. A few days later the stamens reach maturity, the rapid elongation of their filaments causing the anther to hang outside the floret. The anthers split open at the ends, releasing clouds of minute pollen grains in their thousands. Grass pollen is small, spherical and floats in air. If a pollen grain is caught in the brush-like processes of a suitable stigma it germinates by producing a pollen tube which carries the male gametes through the stigma to fertilise the female ovule. This can be a monumental journey for the microscopic pollen tube: for example, in maize (*Zea mais*) the silky threads through which the pollen tube grows may be more than 20 cm long.

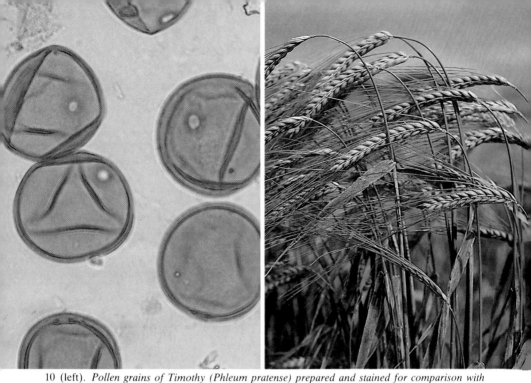

10 (left). *Pollen grains of Timothy (Phleum pratense) prepared and stained for comparison with pollen grains preserved in peat.*
11 (right). *A crop of barley (Hordeum sativum), with distinctive nodding heads and long awns. Although highly cultivated, barley retains many features of its wild relatives.*

Many grasses are annuals, completing their entire life cycle in a single year. A few, including certain of the bromes (*Bromus* species), are biennial, having a first year of exclusively vegetative growth, followed by further vegetative growth and flowering in the second year. The majority of the most familiar grasses are perennials, individual plants surviving for two to many years with a proportion of their growing shoots producing flowers in any one year. After a shoot has flowered it invariably dies back. In many bamboos this has dramatic consequences since flowering occurs at relatively long intervals and is co-ordinated throughout the range of the species. In *Phyllostachys bambusoides*, a bamboo of Chinese origin, records show that flowering occurs at intervals of about 120 years, a cycle that is maintained even in plants cultivated in widely scattered botanic gardens. The staple diet of the giant panda is a bamboo genus (*Fargesia*) which flowers and dies every eight to nine years, causing periodic severe shortages of food which further imperil these endangered animals.

In most grasses the flowering shoot begins to lose its green coloration and dry out as the grains ripen. The grains of many grasses are dispersed simply by falling from the parent plant. Others, including many weedy tropical grasses, are dispersed by catching in the fur of animals. Where very long awns are present these may help in the dispersal and even the burying of the grain. Some awns are jointed with a fine, straight, pointed tip and a broader basal region which coils and uncoils depending upon its moisture content; as the moisture content varies during the day the grains are twisted around and pushed into crevices in the ground. The backward pointing hairs of many grass grains help prevent them dislodging from cracks in the earth.

Grasses are variable in their ecological preferences, some growing almost anywhere whilst others are restricted to quite specific habitats and, as a result, may not be widely encountered. The following chapters trace the history of grasses in the British landscape and describe some of the common grasses under headings of the habitats they favour.

History of grasslands

Grasses are in evidence almost everywhere in Britain and in places they even dominate the vegetation. In many parts the most extensive grass-covered areas are fields. Whether they contain cereals, grazing livestock or a crop of hay, all are clearly the result of human activity. There are few places in Britain where the vegetation we see today has not been shaped by mankind through the centuries. Even the grassy downlands of rolling chalk hills are a form of vegetation maintained only by grazing animals, mainly sheep and rabbits. Without constant cropping, shrubs and trees could become established and the open downs would gradually revert to woodland. Only such places as upland moors, salt marshes and sand dunes, where environmental factors limit the development of woodland, sustain natural forms of grass-dominated vegetation.

As the ice ages came to an end about eight thousand years ago, the glaciers gradually retreated, producing abundant meltwater and exposing the bare earth to colonising plants. Close to the retreating ice, a tundra vegetation similar to that in arctic regions, with grasses and sedges, became established. We can trace the history of the recolonisation that occurred as a warmer climate brought the last ice age to a close, by extracting and identifying pollen grains and plant fragments preserved in peat and other sediments. The proportions of the different pollen types present in the peat provide a continuous record of the changing identity and abundance of plant life. From this record we know that although the tundra vegetation at first contained no trees, woody species such as the dwarf birch (*Betula nana*) and alpine willow (*Salix herbacea*) were present. As the climate became warmer the grass-dominated tundra was rapidly replaced by an invasion of forest-forming trees. First to appear were birches (*Betula* species), Scots pine (*Pinus sylvestris*) and hazel (*Corylus avellana*). Trees with a greater requirement for warmth arrived later and forests of elms (*Ulmus* species), oaks (*Quercus* species), limes (*Tilia*), alder (*Alnus glutinosa*) and other trees were established over most of Britain five to six thousand years ago. The forests were not completely continuous and in many places patches of heath, moorland and marsh provided more open habitats better suited for the growth of grasses. Grasses also dominated, then as now, on coastal dunes and cliffs where other forms of vegetation cannot grow.

Forest clearance originally opened up land for cultivation and provided cut foliage as a feed for livestock. Amongst the earliest cereal crops were varieties of wheat (*Triticum* species) and barley (*Hordeum* species) derived from wild species occurring in the Middle East. These crops have been improved during centuries of cultivation by selection of the high-yielding, disease-resistant varieties (figure 11). Although this process of selection is now a precise science in which desirable characteristics are genetically built in to new varieties, it began simply by early farmers conserving good grain to sow in successive years. The earliest cultivated wheat was einkorn (*Triticum monococcum*), which probably developed as a natural mutation from one of the wild wheats. Einkorn is a diploid plant, that is within each of its cells it has two sets of chromosomes (the structures within each cell that contain the encoded genetic blueprint of the organism). It was superseded by emmer (*Triticum dicoccum*), a tetraploid wheat, with four sets of chromosomes per cell, which produced higher yields. From archaeological finds of its seed grains we know that emmer was cultivated in Britain until the sixth century AD. In more recent times a hexaploid species, bread wheat (*Triticum aestivum*), has become one of the most important crops worldwide. Other cultivated cereals have similarly complex lineages. To see just how much the size

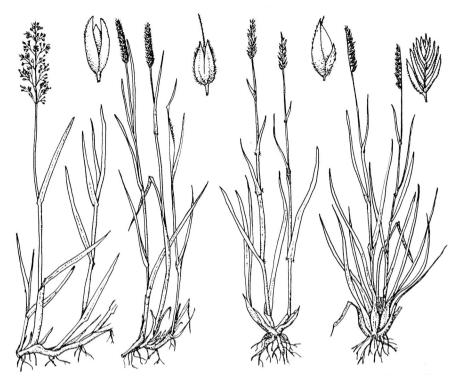

12. *Grasses of meadows and pastures: (left to right) creeping bent (Agrostis stolonifera), 8-40 cm; meadow fox-tail (Alopecurus pratensis), 30-120 cm; sweet vernal-grass (Anthoxanthum odoratum), 10-100 cm; crested dog's-tail (Cynosurus cristatus), 10-75 cm.*

and density of the heads have been increased, it is an interesting exercise to compare the details of cultivated cereals with their wild relatives. Wheat is quite closely related to the couches (*Agropyron* species) whilst wall barley (*Hordeum murinum*) and wild oat (*Avena fatua*) belong to the same genera as their cultivated counterparts.

Pastures and meadows

A very large proportion of the countryside consists of fields, and grasses are clearly the dominant plants which grow in them. Setting aside the vast areas used for the cultivation of cereals and relatively smaller areas taken up by crops of other vegetables, the remaining fields are of interest for the plants they contain. Two types of field may be distinguished, although the use to which a given plot of land is put may vary considerably over the years. In some meadows a crop of hay is harvested, while other pastures are used for grazing livestock. In either case the range of grasses present may be more or less natural and dictated by factors such as the type of soil and the drainage of land or may include species which have been deliberately cultivated. A range of grasses is normally present, even when the spectrum of species represented has been altered to favour the more palatable and faster-growing ones; so meadows and pastures are an obvious place to begin to get to know grasses. Many of the commonest species, including the selection described here (figures 12, 14, 21), will soon become familiar and many will be

13 (above left). *Sheep's fescue (Festuca ovina), a compact chalk downland grass.*

14 (above right). *Inflorescence of cocksfoot (Dactylis glomerata) at time of pollen release.*

15 (below left). *Marram grass (Ammophila arenaria) on sand dunes.*

16 (below right). *Common quaking-grass (Briza media).*

17 (above left). *Wood small-reed (Calamagrostis epigejos) growing at the side of a large lake.*

18 (above right). *Crested dog's-tail (Cynosurus cristatus).*

19 (below left). *Meadow fox-tail (Alopecurus pratensis).*

20 (below right). *Wood brome (Bromus ramosus) growing in a damp oak woodland.*

recognisable again when found in other situations.

Creeping bent (*Agrostis stolonifera*), for instance, is one of the commonest grasses found in fields but will also be encountered in open woodland, downland and in such diverse coastal habitats as salt marshes, cliffs and sand dunes. In some of these locations the plants are genetically different forms adapted to slightly different ecological conditions. Creeping bent is a perennial grass, growing to about 40 cm, which spreads extensively by means of its horizontal, green, leafy stolons and roots at the nodes to form a continuous turf. This property is desirable in some circumstances — it makes the dwarf coastal forms suitable for lawns — but can be a problem in others: it enables the grass to spread and displace more palatable species in pastures. The leaves are slightly bluish green and the ligules membranous, pointed and up to 6 mm long. The inflorescences are panicles with relatively short branches, held upright when the flowering shoot first extends and later spreading. Unlike many other species of bent, the lemmas lack awns.

Meadow fox-tail (*Alopecurus pratensis*) is another very common grass which spreads by short rhizomes and grows to about 120 cm. The leaves are rolled in bud, the old leaf sheaths turning purplish brown, and the ligules are membranous, square-topped and about 3 mm long. The inflorescences are panicles with such short branches that they look like dense spikes. Superficially they have a distinct resemblance to those of Timothy (*Phleum pratense*), which grows in similar places. The inflorescences of meadow fox-tail are softer to the touch and slightly more tapered towards the tip than those of Timothy. Close examination reveals that the former has prominent awns which arise from the bases of the lemmas and protrude well beyond the ends of the glumes, whilst Timothy has only very short awns which arise from the tips of the glumes. Meadow fox-tail has a preference for moist habitats and will often be found in the least well drained parts of a field (figure 8) or in low-lying damp fields such as water meadows. It is one of the earliest-flowering grasses in Britain and comes into flower from the end of April through to July.

Sweet vernal-grass (*Anthoxanthum odoratum*) flowers during the same period. It can grow to about 100 cm but is variable in form and may often be significantly smaller, especially in exposed situations. The leaves are rather soft and hairy with a tuft of straight white hairs at the junction with the sheath. The ligules are toothed and vary in size up to about 6 mm. The inflorescences are spike-like panicles but are much less dense and regular than either Timothy or meadow fox-tail. Sweet vernal-grass has a distinctive smell when dried or when the stems are mown. This grassy fragrance is due to the presence of a substance called coumarin which has a bitter taste and renders the grass unpalatable to livestock. The grass was formerly sown in meadows and pastures because of its sweet smell. The practice has now been discontinued.

Crested dog's-tail (*Cynosurus cristatus*) is a rather wiry-stemmed, perennial grass growing to 75 cm and particularly common in old fields. The leaves are low and short, which provides good grazing for sheep, and are folded when in bud. The ligules are membranous, up to 2 mm long and blunt-topped. The inflorescences are very characteristic one-sided spike-like panicles. The spikelets are a mixture of two kinds: conspicuous sterile spikelets with narrow bristle-like glumes and lemmas (figure 12), and three to five flowered fertile ones (not illustrated).

A large and very common grass with conspicuous dense panicles is cocksfoot (*Dactylis glomerata*). It has laterally compressed tillers and leaves which are folded when in bud but which open to broad flat blades with a single central band of motor-tissue. The ligules are conspicuous, being white and growing up to 12 mm long. The panicles are dense (*glomerata* means 'clumped') and are usually purplish in colour.

Yorkshire fog (*Holcus lanatus*) is often regarded as an undesirable weed because it is unpalatable to livestock except when very young. If not grazed heavily enough, it builds up into dense clumps. Despite this, it is sometimes considered a suitable

14

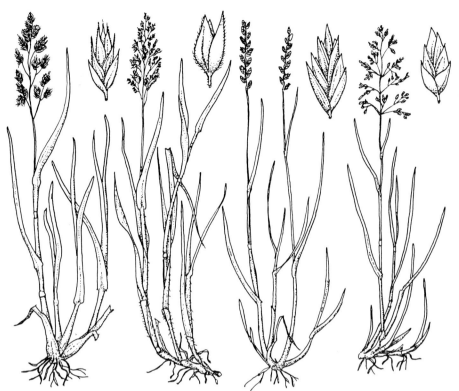

21. *Grasses of meadows and pastures: (left to right) cocksfoot (Dactylis glomerata), 15-140 cm; Yorkshire fog (Holcus lanatus), 20-100 cm; perennial rye-grass (Lolium perenne), 10-90 cm; smooth meadow-grass (Poa pratensis), 10-90 cm.*

grass for grazing, especially in relatively poor land where superior grasses may not grow so well. Yorkshire fog is a softly hairy perennial growing to about 100 cm. The leaves are greyish green with rounded membranous ligules about 4 mm long. The panicles are less dense than those of cocksfoot and softer to the touch but, like those of cocksfoot, they are frequently tinged with purple or may sometimes be whitish.

Perennial rye-grass (*Lolium perenne*), despite its common name, is quite unrelated to the cereal rye. Nevertheless it is a widely cultivated grass, of which many different varieties have been developed for planting in pastures. It grows rapidly and produces high yields of nutritious and palatable foliage. Perennial rye-grass grows to about 90 cm, but much shorter plants will be found flowering in fre-

quently mown areas. The leaves are folded in bud, have small pointed auricles at the junction with the sheath and short membranous ligules about 2 mm long. The inflorescences are erect spikes with the flattened spikelets alternating along opposite sides of the axis.

Another important grass for grazing and haymaking is smooth meadow-grass (*Poa pratensis*), which has been widely cultivated and developed into numerous different strains. Smooth meadow-grass (front cover) is a perennial growing to a maximum of about 90 cm and spreading by slender rhizomes to form a continuous turf. The leaves are soft and covered with minute hairs. The lower leaves are slightly compressed and the ligules are short, rounded and membranous, about 3 mm long. The delicately spreading panicles of this and other species of meadow-grass

15

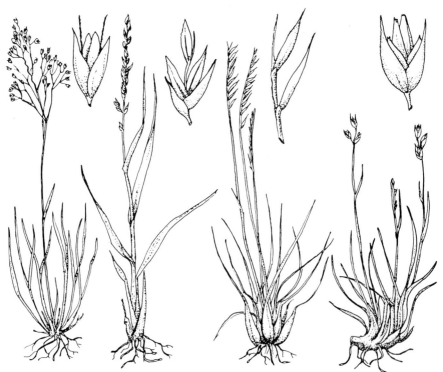

22. Grasses of moors: (left to right) tufted hair-grass (Deschampsia caespitosa), 20-200 cm; purple moor-grass (Molinia caerulea), 15-120 cm; mat-grass (Nardus stricta), 10-50 cm; heath-grass (Sieglingia decumbens), 10-60 cm.

are quite distinctive and are often tinged with pinkish purple. Varieties of meadow-grass are a very common component of seed mixtures used for lawns and sports fields.

Moors and downlands

Moorland dominated by heather (*Calluna vulgaris*) occupies large areas of northern and western Britain where rainfall is high and acidic bedrock is present. Such vegetation may occur naturally above the tree-line on mountains but elsewhere is the result of clearing and grazing what was once largely oak woodland.

Some of the common moorland grasses (figure 22) are found in many other habitats. Tufted hair-grass (*Deschampsia caespitosa*), for example, may be found in wet, marshy ground from sea level to the tops of our highest mountains. It is a perennial grass, growing to 200 cm high and capable of forming large tussocks which are the source of an alternative common name, tussock grass. Tufted hair-grass can be a serious weed in wet fields and once it becomes established it soon becomes too tough for livestock to graze. The narrow, acutely pointed ligules, up to 15 mm long, are a distinctive feature. The loose panicles are large and silvery with two-flowered spikelets. A closely related species, wavy hair-grass (*Deschampsia flexuosa*), is also common on moors. It is a smaller plant with bristle-like leaves which does not form tussocks and is much less aggressive as a weed.

Another common moorland grass, pur-

16

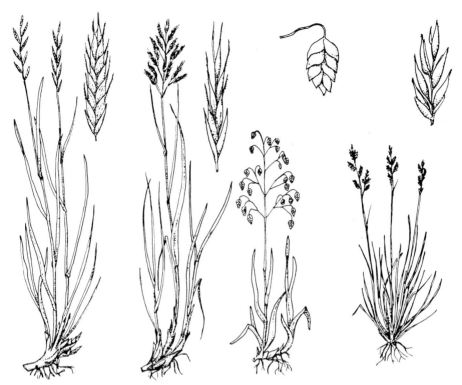

23. *Grasses of calcareous downland: (left to right) tor grass (Brachypodium pinnatum), 30-120 cm; upright brome (Bromus erectus), 40-120 cm; common quaking-grass (Briza media), 15-75 cm; sheep's fescue (Festuca ovina), 5-60 cm.*

ple moor-grass (*Molinia caerulea*), also forms large tussocks and is poor grazing except when very young. It grows to about 120 cm and has narrow tapering leaves. The ligules consist of short hairs. The inflorescences are panicles which vary considerably in the length of the branches. Their purple coloration provides the common name of the grass. Purple moor-grass grows in a wide variety of damp situations including poorly drained fenland and marshes.

Mat-grass (*Nardus stricta*) is a very distinctive, small perennial plant which also grows in particularly wet moorland. Mat-grass reaches about 50 cm in height and has greyish-green, hard, bristle-like leaves with short, blunt membranous ligules about 2 mm long. The erect spikes have all the spikelets arranged in two rows along one side of the axis. Mat-grass takes its name from the almost con-

tinuous carpet it often forms over extensive areas, particularly when growing over peat.

Heath-grass (*Sieglingia decumbens*) has a similar habit but does not form such extensive continuous stands. It is a perennial plant growing to about 60 cm and, like mat-grass, has rather narrow leaves. These differ, however, in being bluntly tipped rather than acute and having ligules which comprise a fringe of short hairs. The inflorescences are small panicles of up to about a dozen spikelets. The flowers never open fully and self-pollination occurs while they are still closed.

It is common in moorland for other grass-like plants to be found. Sedges such as cotton-grasses (*Eriophorum* species) and deer grass (*Trichophorum caespitosum*) may be more numerous than true grasses in many places.

17

In contrast with the rather monotonous vegetation of moors, the downland flora of alkaline chalk hills is enormously rich and diverse. These too are man-made habitats, few of which have included grassland for more than four thousand years and many for considerably less.

Quite a number of different grasses can be found on chalk downs and only a few of the commonest are introduced here (figure 23). Tor grass (*Brachypodium pinnatum*) is a tall, conspicuous perennial, growing to about 120 cm, which frequently stands out from the shorter turf. One reason why it stands out where other grasses have been cropped short is that it is unpalatable. Consequently it is often ignored by sheep and cattle in favour of other grasses such as sheep's fescue (*Festuca ovina*). This allows tor grass to spread, particularly when grazing pressure is generally light, and in many areas it is becoming locally dominant. With the decline of downland sheep farming in the twentieth century, rabbits have become increasingly important in grazing chalk grassland and preventing the spread of invading shrubs. The reduction in rabbit populations as a result of myxomatosis is thought to have been one factor contributing to the spread of tor grass.

Upright brome (*Bromus erectus*) is a similar-sized grass, growing to about 120 cm, and also spreads into undergrazed chalk grassland, although less aggressively than tor grass. The leaves are tough and rather rough, the ligules are membranous, up to 3 mm long and slightly toothed. As in other bromes, the leaf sheaths are tubular and closed. The inflorescences are panicles, which at once distinguishes upright brome from tor grass, which has racemes of short-stalked spikelets.

Amongst the smaller and more delicate grasses of chalk are the quaking-grasses (*Briza* species), which sometimes grow in other locations such as poor grassland. Three species occur in Britain and all possess the distinctive nodding spikelets which make them popular in dried flower arrangements. The common quaking-grass (figure 16) is a perennial plant growing to about 50 cm and occasionally taller (up to 75 cm) whereas the other two species are annuals. The leaves are green and hairless with bluntly pointed tips and short membranous ligules. The characteristic pendulous spikelets are arranged in loose panicles. This grass is so distinctive and attractive that common quaking-grass has become known by numerous different common names, including quaker grass, lady's hair-grass, trembling grass, cow quakes and didder.

The most abundant and characteristic of all downland grasses is sheep's fescue (*Festuca ovina*) (figure 13). This perennial species has permanently rolled, needle-shaped leaves with rounded auricles and extremely short ligules. The inflorescences are erect panicles, often with a purplish coloration. It grows to a height of 60 cm. A close relative, red fescue (*Festuca rubra*), is agriculturally important for grazing livestock and is grown in lawns and sports fields. This species spreads by means of slender rhizomes, which are absent in sheep's fescue. Another way of telling the two apart is to pull off a leaf for close comparison. Those of sheep's fescue, although tightly rolled and cylindrical, can be unrolled, whereas the leaves of red fescue are continuously sealed cylinders.

Coastal grasses

Coastal habitats are very diverse, ranging from rocky near-vertical cliffs, to salt marshes, shingle beaches and sand dunes. Although each of these habitats has its own range of salt-tolerant plants, a selection of the commonest coastal grasses is discussed here (figures 15, 24, 25).

The shifting wind-blown sands of dune systems provide an unstable and adverse habitat where the ability of a few species of grass to thrive is conspicuous. Dunes build up where sand is temporarily stabilised by the presence of these grasses, which consequently must contend with frequent burial. Almost all sand-dune grasses have fast-growing rhizomes or stolons which can spread rapidly to the surface of the dune.

On the seaward side of many dune

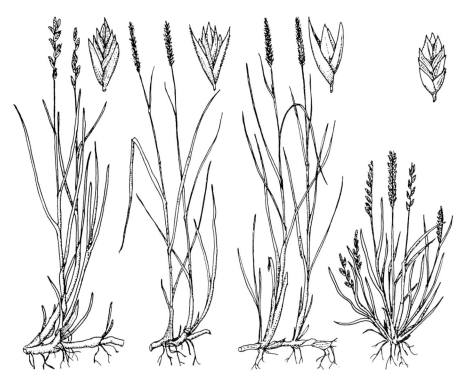

24. *Grasses of coasts and dunes: (left to right) sand couch (Agropyron junceiforme), 20-60 cm; lyme grass (Elymus arenarius), 60-200 cm; marram grass (Ammophila arenaria), 50-120 cm; stiff sand-grass (Catapodium marinum), 5-20 cm.*

systems the nearest grass to the sea is usually the most salt-tolerant dune grass of all, sand couch (*Agropyron junceiforme*). This is a perennial plant growing to about 60 cm, whose bluish green colour is explained by the presence of a waxy bloom which helps protect against damage by salt spray. The leaf blades may be flattened but often roll up, folding along a dozen or so lines of motor-tissue. Rolled leaves are also a protection against the harsh climatic conditions of the dunes. By reducing the amount of water lost by evaporation from the leaves, rolling helps the grass to survive in a habitat which is so well drained that little fresh water is available to the roots. Sand couch is able to grow up through a depth of only about 1.5 metres of accumulating sand and consequently forms relatively low dune systems. Other dune-forming grasses,

especially marram grass (*Ammophila arenaria*), can grow up through much thicker layers of sand and form larger dunes. Sand couch has short, rounded membranous ligules; the inflorescences are spikes with two rows of alternating spikelets. The flowering season extends from June to August.

Lyme grass (*Elymus arenarius*) is a second major dune-building grass, which forms large clumps up to 200 cm tall. It often grows mixed with marram, the principal dune former (figure 15), which grows to 120 cm high. Like sand couch, both lyme grass and marram have a protective bluish grey waxy sheen but, despite the superficial similarities of their habit and flower spikes, the two can easily be distinguished. Lyme grass has flattened leaf blades with pointed auricles at the base, while those of marram lack auricles and are tightly rolled. Closer

19

examination reveals differences in the inflorescences of the two grasses. Whereas lyme grass has true spikes, the inflorescences of marram are spike-like panicles in which the branches of the inflorescence are extremely short. Marram grass has single-flowered spikelets and lyme grass has three to six flowers in each spikelet. Both species are in flower from June to August. Lyme grass is a more vigorous grower than sand couch and can form substantial dunes but it is only marram grass that can carry on growing through 25 to 30 metres of sand to form major dunes.

A shorter grass (5 to 20 cm high) often found amongst the taller clumps of marram and lyme grass is stiff sand-grass (*Catapodium marinum*). This is an annual plant so it completes its entire life cycle from germination to seed-setting in a single year. Its strategy is different from the dune-building grasses and their constant struggle to avoid burial. The stiff sand-grass relies on rapidly completing its life cycle during the relative stability of a single growing season. It is not restricted to sand dunes, however, and occurs in a variety of coastal habitats including rocky cliffs and shingly beaches. Stiff sand-grass has hairless leaves with blunt-tipped membranous ligules up to 3 mm long. It flowers from May to July and has short rather spike-like panicles; the spikelets lie in two rows on one side of the shoot, giving a rather distinctive appearance to the inflorescences. The stiff sand-grass is a close relative of the meadow-grasses (*Poa* species) and was formerly classified in their genus. The differences between the two genera involve fine details of flower structure, *Catapodium* having rounded hairless lemmas and *Poa* keeled, hairy ones.

A second annual grass which leads a similar precarious existence in the changing sand dunes and on shingle beaches is sand cat's-tail (*Phleum arenarium*). This compact grass rarely exceeds 25 cm in height. The leaves are short and relatively broad, and the upper leaf sheaths are rather inflated, giving a slightly swollen appearance. The ligules are membranous, acute and about 7 mm long. The inflorescences are immediately reminiscent of Timothy (*Phleum*

pratense), a more familiar relative, and an alternative common name is sand Timothy. The species name of sand cat's-tail is the same as that of marram and many other coastal plants: *arenarium* means literally 'of the sands'. Many other coastal plants have specific names such as *maritimum* or *marinum*, indicative of their habitat.

Sand dunes are a much more popular location for seaside relaxation than another coastal habitat which nevertheless contains many interesting plants. Salt marshes are very gently sloping muddy areas which are regularly submerged during the highest tides of the year. Salt marshes contain a special plant community ranging from fully submerged flowering plants such as grass-wracks (*Zostera* species), which are not really grasses at all, to the succulent stemmed glasswort (*Salicornia* species). Some unusual and interesting grasses are adapted to life in the salt marshes. Sea hard-grass (*Parapholis strigosa*) is another annual species. It may grow as tall as 40 cm but frequently forms much shorter clumps, especially when it strays into drier coastal locations such as sand dunes. The leaves are waxy and greyish green in colour, with very short, slightly jagged, membranous ligules. The inflorescences are narrow, inconspicuous spikes which appear almost cylindrical before the flowers open. As the sunken, single-flowered spikelets open they fold until they project outwards from the inflorescence. A less common relative which favours drier coastal situations is curved sea hard-grass (*Parapholis incurva*). It can be recognised by its shorter spikes, which are curved rather than straight. The distinctive spikes with sunken spikelets present in the two species provide an easy means of identifying the genus *Parapholis*.

A much larger grass of coastal mudflats and salt marshes is common cordgrass (*Spartina anglica*), which grows up to 130 cm tall. This is a perennial plant which spreads by thick, fleshy rhizomes buried in the mud. The ligules (figure 3d) are very distinctive, being composed of hairs 2 to 3 mm in length. The leaf blades are broad and flat or rolled with a hard pointed tip. The panicles are composed of up to about a dozen erect spikes. This grass has an interesting history since it originated as a result of the natural hybridisation of two other *Spartina* species in the late nineteenth century. One parent of the hybrid was cord-grass (*Spartina maritima*), a relatively uncommon salt-marsh grass found at scattered locations in southern Britain. The other was *Spartina alternifolia*, a plant introduced accidentally from North America and first recorded in England in 1829. About forty years later a new species, Townsend's cord-grass (*Spartina x townsendii*), was described from Southampton Water. As with many hybrids, the result of the cross-breeding was a much more vigorous plant, although one which does not produce fertile pollen. Common cord-grass, the most vigorous of all, is thought to have arisen by one more genetic change: a doubling of the chromosome number. Common cord-grass has been planted in many coastal areas to stabilise drifting mud-flats by protecting them from erosion and to reclaim marshy areas from the sea.

Reflexed salt-marsh grass (*Puccinella distans*) is another frequent inhabitant of salt marshes. It is a perennial plant growing to a height of 60 cm with greyish green leaves. The inflorescences are delicate panicles which are held erect as flowering begins and gradually become sharply reflexed.

Wetland grasses

Fresh water is the dominant feature in many very different habitats ranging from marshes to streams, rivers, ponds and lakes. Grasses are a feature of the margins of each of these habitats, some growing partially submerged whilst others float and spread out over the surface of the water. Some of the grasses found around water margins also occur in other damp places, for example the moorland grasses tufted hair-grass and purple moor-grass. There are a number of grasses restricted more narrowly to wetland and a selection of the commoner ones are described here (figures 17 and 26).

Floating fox-tail (*Alopecurus geniculatus*) is a perennial grass 15-45 cm tall, with widely spreading horizontal culms, which roots at the nodes and which sometimes floats in water. The leaves are hairless with slightly inflated sheaths and long membranous ligules, up to 5 mm. The stems are jointed where flowering heads arise and the inflorescences are narrow, spike-like panicles.

Wood small-reed (*Calamagrostis epigejos*) also grows in ditches and around pond margins but has a preference for shady places and so is mainly found in patches of open water within woods. It grows to 200 cm, spreading by rhizomes and often forming large tussocks (figure 17). The leaves are long and coarse with rather long, membranous, slightly toothed ligules up to 12 mm long. The inflorescences are large panicles with erect branches. The spikelets are narrow and one-flowered, and a distinctive feature visible when they are examined closely is that the lemmas are surrounded by fine straight hairs almost as long as the glumes. A number of related *Calamagrostis* species grow in similar habitats. One extremely rare relative is the Scottish small-reed (*Calamagrostis scotica*), known only from bogs in Caithness (Highland Region). This is one of a relatively small number of endemic British plant species, that is it grows nowhere outside Britain.

Floating sweet-grass (*Glyceria fluitans*) is another perennial grass, growing to about 100 cm, which is found in the shallow water of ponds, ditches and rivers. Like floating fox-tail, the plant has erect aerial stems and horizontal culms which sometimes float on the surface of the water. The leaves are hairless with purplish, tubular sheaths and very long, acutely pointed ligules up to 15 mm. The inflorescences are long panicles which are spreading when in flower but later become contracted and nodding. The grass often grows in low-lying water meadows where it is avidly consumed by grazing livestock.

One of the most important aquatic grasses is the common reed (*Phragmites communis*), which covers extensive areas of swamp and marsh. It is one of the

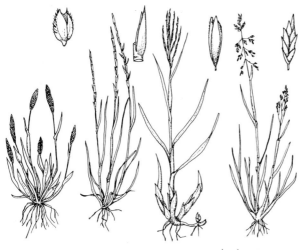

25. *Grasses of salt marshes and shingles: (left to right) sand cat's-tail (Phleum arenarium), 5-25 cm; sea hard-grass (Parapholis strigosa), 10-40 cm; common cord-grass (Spartina anglica), 30-130 cm; reflexed salt-marsh grass (Puccinella distans), 10-60 cm.*

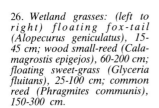

26. *Wetland grasses: (left to right) floating fox-tail (Alopecurus geniculatus), 15-45 cm; wood small-reed (Calamagrostis epigejos), 60-200 cm; floating sweet-grass (Glyceria fluitans), 25-100 cm; common reed (Phragmites communis), 150-300 cm.*

world's most widely distributed plants and can be found in appropriate habitats throughout the temperate regions and in the tropics. Common reed contributes significantly to the peat deposits which accumulate in fenland areas. As the peat builds up, previously wet areas of land progressively become drier and habitable to a range of different plants, which eventually displace the reeds. The deposits of peat left behind provide a useful source of organic material for improving the soil in gardens. They also preserve, in the form of pollen grains and other plant fragments, a record of the history of the swamp from its time as an open-water community dominated by reeds and other grasses to its invasion by sedges, trees and shrubs.

Common reed has the distinction of being the tallest British grass, growing to 3 metres. It spreads by means of thick rhizomes which give rise at intervals to rather solid, erect, unbranched stems. The leaves are broad and greyish green, tapering to fine points. The ligule is a fringe of short hairs. Inflorescences are very large, dense panicles, often tinged with purple. Like the wood small-reed, the lemmas have fine hairs, rather silky in the common reed, and longer than the surrounding glumes.

Woodland grasses

The woodland habitat is not a rich one for grasses. Two reasons for this are that most grasses require the higher light intensity of open spaces and that their dependence on wind pollination is less effective in woods, where air currents are reduced. The most important factor is probably light, and it can often be seen that grasses are fairly numerous and varied around the margins of a wood but soon become scarcer and restricted to just a few species (figure 27) further into the wood. Around the margins of a wood the grasses present are just those of the surrounding habitat; those that live in the shady areas are specialised wood dwellers which are rarely found in full light.

Wood false-brome (*Brachypodium sylvaticum*) is one such woodland grass (figure 27), the species name *sylvaticum* meaning 'of the woods'. Like most woodland grasses, wood false-brome is also found in shady hedgerows and along the verges of lanes with overhanging trees. Once established, it can continue to grow after the shading trees have been felled and so it is sometimes found as a relic of cleared woodland. The common name of this grass emphasises its resemblance to one of the bromes (*Bromus* species), to which it is not related. The two genera of grasses are similar in habit but in the inflorescences of false-bromes the spikelets are borne on very much shorter stalks than those of the true bromes.

Wood false-brome is a perennial plant which grows to about 90 cm tall and has erect culms differing from the well developed rhizomes of its chalk downland relative, tor grass (*Brachypodium pinna-*

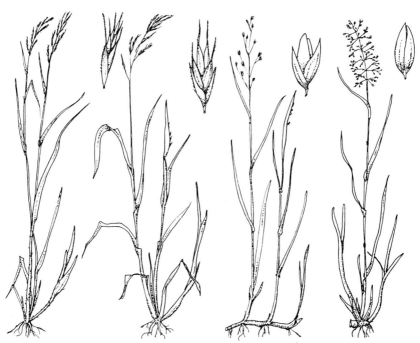

27. *Woodland grasses: (left to right) wood false-brome (Brachypodium sylvaticum), 30-90 cm; wood brome (Bromus ramosus), 45-190 cm; wood melick (Melica uniflora), 20-60 cm; wood millet (Milium effusum), 45-180 cm.*

23

tum). The stems and undersides of the leaves are covered with fine, spreading hairs. The ligules are membranous, bluntly rounded and about 5 or 6 mm long. The inflorescence is a spike-like raceme of rather nodding spikelets. The glumes are slightly hairy and the lemmas each have a long rough awn about 10 to 12 mm long arising from their tips. This is another point of difference from the bromes, in which the awns arise from the back of the lemmas rather than from their tips. The flowering season extends from July to August.

Wood brome (*Bromus ramosus*) flowers during the same period but, as mentioned above, can be distinguished by the long, delicately curving, branched stalks on which the spikelets are borne. These give the inflorescences a loose and nodding appearance. Wood brome is a tall (190 cm) perennial grass with dark green leaves. The sheaths of the leaves are cylindrical and covered with fine backward-pointing hairs, whilst the leaves themselves are finely hairy. The ligules are membranous, rounded to slightly jagged and about 6 mm long. A rare relative of wood brome, found in woods and shady places on calcareous soil, is the lesser hairy brome (*Bromus benekenii*). This grows mainly in beech woods and can be distinguished by its hairless leaf blades, although the sheaths are hairy, and by fewer flowers in each spikelet. Other species of brome tend to favour more open habitats, several being weeds of arable land and waste ground. Another fairly common woodland grass which resembles both the wood brome and wood false-brome is giant fescue (*Festuca gigantea*). This also has rather nodding panicles of spikelets with long awns but can be distinguished by the conspicuous pointed auricles (figure 3b) at the bases of the leaf blades.

Two other common woodland grasses flowering from May to July have distinctive delicate inflorescences, the branches of which each terminate in a single-flowered spikelet.

Wood melick (*Melica uniflora*) is a perennial grass growing to about 60 cm tall, with pale, spreading rhizomes. The leaf sheaths are closed and cylindrical and are often covered with very small reflexed hairs. The ligules are short and membranous. The inflorescences are very loose panicles with few branches and only a few single-flowered spikelets at the ends. This attractive grass often forms an open carpet in shady woods where few other herbaceous plants are found, for example in the dense shade of beech woods. No other member of the genus occurs naturally in Britain.

Wood millet (*Milium effusum*) is a taller perennial, growing up to about 180 cm tall and, like wood melick, is also the sole British representative of its genus. It tends to grow in slightly wetter places than wood melick in beech, ash and oak woods. The leaves are broad and hairless with prominent pointed ligules up to 10 mm long. The panicles have uneven whorls of delicate spreading or slightly deflexed branches. The spikelets are single-flowered.

Further reading

Clapham, A. R.; Tutin, T. G.; and Warburg, E. F. *Flora of the British Isles*. Cambridge University Press, 1962.

Hubbard, C. E. *Grasses*. Penguin Books, 1968.

Keeble-Martin, W. *The Concise British Flora In Colour*. Ebury Press, 1965.

Philips, R. *Grasses, Ferns, Mosses and Lichens of Great Britain and Ireland*. Pan Books, 1980.

Sikula, J. *Grasses*. Hamlyn Books, 1978.

Stokoe, W. J. *The Observer's Book of Grasses, Sedges and Rushes*. Warne, 1958.

ACKNOWLEDGEMENTS
All photographs and drawings are by Stephen Blackmore.